20ᵀᴴ CENTURY WORLD HISTORY FOR KIDS

20th CENTURY WORLD HISTORY FOR Kids

the MAJOR EVENTS THAT SHAPED the PAST and PRESENT

JUDY DODGE CUMMINGS

ROCKRIDGE
PRESS

Series Designer: Michael Patti
Interior and Cover Designer: Elizabeth Zuhl
Art Producer: Sue Bischofberger
Editor: Barbara J. Isenberg
Production Manager: Martin Worthington
Production Editor: Melissa Edeburn

Cover illustration © 2021 Jonathan Ball. Interior illustration © IanDagnall Computing/Alamy, p. 13; INTERFOTO/Alamy, p. 24; Detlev Van Ravenswaay/Science Source, p. 56; Fredrik Skold/Alamy, p. 99.
Photography © Alpha Historica/Alamy, p. 4; Hi-Story/Alamy, p. 5; Library of Congress [no collection specified], pp. 7 and 10; Smith Archive/Alamy, p. 11; Pictorial Press Ltd/Alamy, pp. 16, 28, 57, and 70; Classic Image/Alamy, p. 19; The History Collection/Alamy, p. 20; IanDagnall Computing/Alamy, pp. 25 and 33; Science History Images/Alamy, p. 27; Sueddeutsche Zeitung Photo/Alam, pp. 30 and 36; Everett Collection Inc/Alamy, p. 37; ARCHIVIO GBB/Alamy, p. 39; United States Air Force/Library of Congress, p. 44; INTERFOTO/Alamy, p. 47; BNA Photographic/Alamy, p. 48; Maciej Bledowski/Alamy, p. 50; Maureen Keating/Library of Congress, p. 53; Gary Doak/Alamy, p. 54; World History Archive/Alamy, pp. 59, 68, and 73; mccool/Alamy, p. 64; SIGURD BO BOJESEN/AFP via Getty Images, p. 67; Trinity Mirror/Mirrorpix/Alamy, p. 71; Keystone Press/Alamy, p. 76; Warren K. Leffler/Library of Congress, p. 79; GL Archive/Alamy, p. 80; Carol M. Highsmith/Carol M. Highsmith Archive/Library of Congress, p. 84; REUTERS/Alamy, p. 85; Kim Haughton/Alamy, p. 87; ZUMA Press, Inc./Alamy, p. 90; imageBROKER/Alamy, p. 93; Photo 12/Alamy, p. 94; and CERN/Science Source, p. 96.

ISBN: Print 978-1-64876-761-6 | eBook 978-1-64876-762-3
R0

IN LOVING MEMORY OF MY DAD,
LARRY DODGE, WHO SHOWED ME
THE WORLD, ENCOURAGED
ME TO WRITE, AND INSPIRED MY
LOVE OF HISTORY.

CONTENTS

INTRODUCTION

orld history teaches us what it means to be human. When reading world history, you do not examine just one nation or one civilization. Instead, you explore all humanity. This broad perspective sheds light on how our thoughts, values, and behaviors have changed over time. World history helps us realize how connected we are to everyone else.

Although all past eras have shaped the modern world, the 20th century has had the strongest impact on us today. In a sense, the world became smaller in the 1900s. Changes in transportation and communication brought people from distant lands together in ways that could not have happened in earlier times. Two world wars introduced conflicts that couldn't be constrained to any one region. Millions died or became refugees. National boundaries shifted when the gunfire ended.

In addition to wars, revolutions, and independence movements, large-scale **civil disobedience** erupted on almost every continent in the 20th century. People who were poor or oppressed compared their lot in life to those in the ruling class and decided enough was enough. Some of these resistance movements succeeded, whereas others ended in bloody crackdowns.

Despite the violence, the 20th century was also an era of progress. Scientific advancements helped people survive deadly **pandemics**. New insights led governments to **reform** systems to avoid future economic collapse. Breakthroughs in technology allowed people to explore frontiers in outer space and medicine.

This book presents just some of the most important political, social, and economic events of the 20th century. You can learn about other events by checking the Resources at the back of this book. The past always affects the present. In order to understand the century in which you are living, it is vital to understand what came before. So from the comfort of your couch or your classroom, turn the page and begin your journey back in time.

THE WORLD AT THE TURN OF THE 20th CENTURY

As the 1900s began, people around the world greeted the new century with excitement and hope. Scientific advancements were transforming daily life. Electric lights now brightened rooms instead of oil lamps. Automobiles zoomed past horse-drawn carriages. Crowds packed theaters to watch motion pictures. Educational reforms meant more people than ever before could read and write.

But these changes did not improve everyone's lives. Discontent simmered in many countries.

As the 20th century began in 1901, the United States and Japan began to flex their economic and military muscles. The United States was the world's largest democracy and the most productive. Now the United States wanted global influence, too. Japan had been isolated for centuries, but a reform-minded government opened trade with Western nations.

As New Year festivities ended the 19th century, people dreamed of possibilities. In the new century, some hopes would be fulfilled, others would be dashed.

CHAPTER ONE

1901 TO 1920

The old world and the new world collided in the first two decades of the 20th century. Scientists discovered how time and space interact in the universe. The desire to test humankind's limits sent adventurers to the skies and to the polar ice caps. Innovators built airplanes and automobiles. They invented electricity and X-rays. Once extraordinary, these devices soon became part of everyday life for the rich and middle class.

But as the world modernized and life sped up, many people were left behind. Poor workers in cities and peasants in the country struggled to survive. The wealth difference between rich and poor people grew, leading to resentment. Revolutions erupted in China, Mexico, and Russia. In Europe, tensions simmered just under the surface as ethnic minorities lived under the thumbs of monarchs to whom they felt no loyalty.

European monarchs vied for power. They gobbled up colonies in Latin America, Asia, and Africa. The ranks of armies swelled. Battleships and airplanes rolled off assembly lines. European leaders made defensive **alliances** with neighboring nations and against them. Economic and political tensions made the world a powder keg. All it would take to explode was a spark.

Albert Einstein

Einstein's Theory of Relativity: 1905

In 1905, Albert Einstein published his theory of relativity and transformed the world's understanding of the universe.

As a child growing up in Germany, Einstein struggled in school. Instead of paying attention, he conducted "thought experiments" in his head. When he was 16, he imagined himself chasing down a beam of light. If he could ride alongside it, Einstein figured, the beam would appear frozen.

After earning a degree in physics and mathematics, Einstein took a job as a clerk in Bern, Switzerland.

He still ran thought experiments in his mind. One day while riding the streetcar, Einstein looked at the clock tower looming over the city. He imagined that if the streetcar raced away from the clock at the speed of light, the clock hands would stop. At that moment, Einstein said "a storm broke loose in my mind." It was not light that freezes in space. It was time.

In 1905, Einstein published the theory of relativity. Through mathematical equations, he showed that the laws of physics are the same everywhere, whether someone is on Earth or in outer space. One such law is that the speed of light never changes. A related law is that time and

space are not constant. Time passes more slowly the faster one moves.

Einstein also showed that the faster an object moves, the more massive it becomes. He expressed the relationship between mass and speed with an equation: $E = mc^2$. This means that energy equals mass times the speed of light squared. Einstein used math to prove that there is a lot of energy in mass. The key for future scientists would be to figure out how to convert that mass in order to harness the power of its energy.

Scientists did just that throughout the 20th century. Global Positioning Systems (GPS), nuclear power plants, and electromagnets that bring electricity to homes are just a few developments that Einstein's theory made possible.

LEWIS AND CLARK CENTENNIAL EXPOSITION

The same year that Einstein released his theory of relativity, Portland, Oregon, hosted a world's fair. Twenty-one nations and 16 states showcased marvels of the new century. Nearly 1.6 million people were entertained by blimps, motion pictures, and the first transcontinental auto race. At night, the fair was lit up by another modern invention: electricity.

Soldiers during the Mexican Revolution

The Mexican Revolution: 1910

In 1910, Porfirio Díaz was running for his seventh term as president of Mexico. He had been **dictator** since 1877 and rigged every election. After 30 years, Mexicans had had enough. Businessman Francisco Madero campaigned against Díaz. On the eve of the election, Madero was arrested and Díaz declared himself the winner.

When Madero got out of jail, he called on Mexicans to overthrow Díaz and form a **democratic republic**. The call to arms was taken up by peasants. These **Indigenous** People performed the work that

MEET THE SOLDADERAS

Mexican women were key players in the 1910 revolution. Called soldaderas, some women joined the federal army and others the rebel forces. Most soldaderas were cooks, nurses, and supply smugglers, but other women took up arms. To protect themselves from discrimination, some of these warriors disguised themselves as men. Petra Herrera was one such soldier. She went by the name of Pedro. Well respected for her bravery, Herrera commanded a force of 200 men.

kept Mexico afloat, but Díaz had long ignored their needs. Peasants worked on plantations owned by wealthy landowners. They grew sugar, cotton, coffee, and other crops they could not afford to buy.

Two men with rural roots became leaders of the rebellion. In northern Mexico, Pancho Villa recruited an army of villagers. In the south, Emiliano Zapata led attacks against corrupt local leaders. The slogan of the revolutionaries was "*tierra y libertad*"—land and liberty.

On May 25, 1911, Porfirio Díaz resigned and went into **exile**. Madero was elected president. However, the revolution was not over. Two years later, army commander Victoriano Huerta ordered Madero assassinated and seized power. The rebels refused to accept this. Fighting continued until Huerta had to flee the country.

In 1914, Venustiano Carranza, a landowner in northern Mexico, called a meeting between the rebels and the military to negotiate peace. A new constitution promising land reform and economic rights for the poor was approved in 1917. The people elected Carranza president. However, he ignored the constitution and governed only for the rich. Peasants resumed their rebellion.

Carranza was assassinated in 1920, and fighting continued off and on until 1934. That year, Lázaro Cárdenas was elected president. He finally enacted the reforms for which so many revolutionaries had sacrificed their lives.

PANIC OVER A COMET

Halley's Comet, a snowball of gas and space rocks, is visible from Earth every 76 years. In 1910, astronomers realized Earth would pass through the comet's tail on May 19. People panicked. Churches held prayer vigils. Frauds sold pills they claimed would protect people from the comet's poisonous gas. But when dawn broke on May 20, the world had not ended. Halley's Comet will next return in 2061.

Robert Falcon Scott's expedition group

Race for the South Pole: 1911

By the early 20th century, Antarctica was the last unexplored continent. In 1911, teams led by Roald Amundsen and Robert Falcon Scott raced to reach the South Pole first.

Inuit people in the Arctic had taught Amundsen, an experienced Norwegian explorer, to use dogs to pull sleds over icy terrain.

To transport supplies, Scott, a British naval officer, chose motorized sleds and Siberian ponies, two modes untested in polar conditions.

Amundsen planned every detail of his expedition but was ready to change course if severe weather struck. Scott was less careful. He did not pack enough food and made mistakes plotting his route.

On October 20, the Norwegian crew oot off. The men skied alongside the dogsleds. They made good time. On December 14, the team reached the flat, ice-covered plateau where the South Pole is located. The proud Norwegians hoisted their flag and headed back to base camp.

Meanwhile, the British team was plagued with problems. Blizzards delayed their departure. The

MEET ADA BLACKJACK

In 1921, Ada Blackjack was a poor, young single mother. She signed on as seamstress with a four-man expedition to an island north of Siberia, an important job because the crew needed their fur parkas and mittens kept in good repair. After a year, rations ran out. The supply ship never arrived. In January 1923, three men left to walk for help. They were never seen again. Blackjack cared for the fourth man, but he died in June, leaving her alone. She survived by shooting seals until a rescue ship arrived in August. Newspapers labeled Blackjack the female Robinson Crusoe.

motorized sleds kept stalling, and the ponies died. The crew had to pull the heavy supply sleds themselves.

The British team reached the South Pole on January 16. With crushing disappointment, they saw the Norwegian flag blowing in the wind. There was nothing to do but return to base camp.

But the men were low on rations. One by one, the crew fell sick from hunger, hypothermia, scurvy, and frostbite. Two men died. The temperature dropped to 40 degrees below zero (Fahrenheit). A blizzard trapped the surviving men in their tent only 11 miles from base camp. The following spring, a search party found their frozen bodies.

The race to the South Pole was a lesson in leadership. The Norwegians proved that flexibility, experience, and detailed planning are more important than pure courage.

FOOT BINDING BANNED

Foot binding was a centuries-old custom in China thought to make women attractive. A girl's toes were bent underneath the soles of her feet and tied in place. As the feet grew, the bones were repeatedly broken until the deformity was permanent. In 1912, the Chinese government banned foot binding.

Painting of the assassination of the Archduke

The Assassination of Archduke Franz Ferdinand: 1914

On June 28, 1914, the murder of one man sparked World War I.

In the early 20th century, no single power dominated Europe. Instead, countries made defensive **treaties** and increased their military might. This meant that an attack on one nation would lead to revenge by that nation's allies. Two opposing camps emerged: The Triple Alliance included Austria-Hungary, Germany, and Italy, and the Triple Entente was made up of Britain, France, and Russia.

In June, Archduke Franz Ferdinand headed to Sarajevo, Bosnia, for official events. Ferdinand was the heir to the throne of Austria-Hungary. Austria-Hungary had seized Bosnia in 1908. This land grab angered people in neighboring Serbia. They considered Bosnia part of Serbia. On learning of Ferdinand's visit, some Bosnian students plotted to kill him.

The Black Hand, a terrorist group linked to the Serbian army, gave the students bombs and guns.

On June 28, Ferdinand and his wife were riding in an open-topped car through Sarajevo. The driver of the archduke's car took the wrong street. As the car slowed down to turn around, 19-year-old Gavrilo Princip whipped out his pistol and fired twice, killing Ferdinand and his wife.

The murder of Ferdinand spiraled into war. One month later, Austria-Hungary declared war on Serbia. Germany, Russia, France, Belgium, Montenegro, and Britain were pulled into the conflict as they came to the aid of their allies. Over the next four years, other nations became involved in what was called "The Great War." More than 20 million soldiers died in the conflict. The war destroyed the royal dynasties of Germany, Austria-Hungary, Russia, and Turkey and unleashed revolutionary forces in Russia. The aftermath also led, some 20 years later, to World War II.

A PATRIOTIC PIGEON

On October 4, 1918, a homing pigeon named Cher Ami saved 200 soldiers with the United States 77th Infantry. The men were trapped behind enemy lines in France. Nearby American troops thought the trapped men were German soldiers and began to fire on them. Despite being shot in the breast and wing, Cher Ami delivered this message from the trapped Americans: "OUR ARTILLERY IS DROPPING A BARRAGE DIRECTLY ON US. FOR HEAVENS SAKE STOP IT." Cher Ami was awarded a medal for bravery.

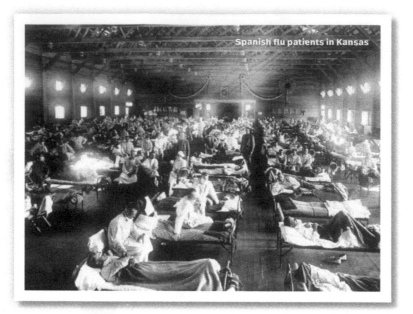
Spanish flu patients in Kansas

The Spanish Flu: 1918

As World War I raged across Europe in 1918, something new began to kill soldiers: not a bullet or a bomb, but a flu.

After the illness was detected in Spain in February, journalists nicknamed it the Spanish Flu. However, the virus probably originated on a US Army base in Kansas. When soldiers from this base reached the battlefields of Europe, they brought the disease along. Soon, the so-called Spanish Flu had gone global.

U.S. government leaders worried more about winning the war than stopping the disease. Officials prevented newspapers from publishing articles that might alarm people, so citizens did not realize how easily the flu spread. Factory workers toiled on crowded floors to produce war materials. People gathered for parades to support the troops. Meanwhile, the virus changed. By September, the flu was not only very contagious but also very deadly.

People with the flu reported skull-splitting headaches and bone-rattling fevers. Their lungs filled with fluid. Their skin turned blue. October was the deadliest month. Fourteen percent of the people living in the Fiji Islands died. The death rate among victims in Chicago jumped to 40 percent. Cape Town, South Africa, ran out of coffins.

Finally, government leaders acted. Cities closed down bars and theaters. Schools excluded sick

MEET WOODROW WILSON

In 1919, United States President Woodrow Wilson was negotiating the **treaty** to end World War I. He wanted to create a fair and lasting peace, but in April, Wilson fell gravely ill with the Spanish Flu. The president grew confused and had hallucinations. With Wilson too weak to fight for a fair peace, the leaders of France and Britain wrote a treaty that punished Germany severely. This flawed treaty helped lead to World War II.

students. People wore gauze masks in public. But it was too little, too late. In just two years, the Spanish Flu killed an estimated 50 million people around the world.

In 2020, a virus called COVID-19 caused another deadly pandemic. Although a century had passed since the Spanish Flu, the two pandemics have similarities. Just as in 1918, some modern leaders did little to protect their citizens. Both diseases easily jumped borders because some people didn't wear masks or quarantine.

TARZAN OF THE APES PREMIERS

Hollywood released *Tarzan of the Apes* in 1918. This silent film was different from other movies of the time. Instead of being filmed on a Hollywood set, it was shot in the swamps of Louisiana. Typically, white actors with their faces painted portrayed Black characters. But in *Tarzan*, Black Americans were allowed on camera. Although movie tickets usually cost 7 cents at the time, audiences had to pay $1.50 to see *Tarzan*.

World leaders at Versailles

The Treaty of Versailles and the League of Nations: 1919

The guns of World War I finally fell silent on November 11, 1918, when both sides signed a cease-fire. In January 1919, world leaders gathered at the Palace of Versailles in Paris, France, to negotiate a permanent peace. The conference was dominated by the United States, Great Britain, France, and Italy. Representatives from the defeated nations were not allowed to attend.

Marguerite de Witt-Schlumberger was a French **activist.** She organized the Inter-Allied Women's Conference in Paris while the Treaty of Versailles was being negotiated. Schlumberger asked world leaders to include women's political and economic rights in the final treaty. The leaders refused, saying women's rights were a matter each country had to decide for itself. Schlumberger died in 1924, 20 years before French women won the right to vote.

United States President Woodrow Wilson came to the conference with a 14-point plan to strengthen democracy around the world. Wilson also wanted to create a "League of Nations"—an international organization that would give countries a place to settle disputes peacefully and avoid war.

But the leaders of Great Britain, France, and Italy ignored Wilson's plan. They wanted to punish Germany. The final agreement was called the Treaty of Versailles, and it was harsh. Germany was forced to accept full responsibility for starting the war.

The victorious nations also charged Germany $33 billion in war damages and seized 10 percent of German territory.

The British, French, and Italian leaders did agree to form the League of Nations. But now the United States balked. United States senators must agree to a treaty before a president can sign it into law. Senators feared that an international body like the League would pull the United States into Europe's problems. So the United States never signed the Treaty of Versailles and never joined the League of Nations. Without the support of the world's newest superpower, the League was doomed to failure.

Germans were infuriated by the terms of the treaty. People looked for leaders who would redeem Germany's pride, setting the stage for the rise of the Nazi Party and the onset of World War II.

BABE RUTH FOR SALE

Throughout World War I, baseball player Babe Ruth entertained Americans. On December 26, 1919, the Boston Red Sox traded Ruth to the New York Yankees for the historic price of $100,000. For 15 seasons, Ruth broke records in home runs and ticket sales.

CHAPTER TWO

1921

TO

1940

In the 1920s, global economies boomed. The
United States emerged from World War I as
the world's biggest producer. Although it took
longer for Europe to recover from the war,
by the mid-1920s, the automotive, radio, and

commercial aviation industries had spurred economic growth.

But in the 1930s, that boom went bust. The **stock market** in the United States crashed in 1929, sending the world's richest nation into a tailspin. The Great Depression began, spreading from the United States to the rest of the world. Global production slowed. International trade plunged. Unemployment rates soared.

Both decades saw new **ideologies** spread. Indian activists, inspired by leader Mohandas Gandhi, began a campaign of civil disobedience against British rule. **Boycotts**, protests, and marches eventually led Great Britain to grant India its independence. Revolutions in Russia and China ended in civil wars. The victor in both countries was **communism**, and so the new nations of the Soviet Union and the People's Republic of China were founded. In Germany, a far-right political party rose to power in the 1930s. Led by Adolf Hitler, this Nazi Party viewed both communists and Jews as the enemy. Determined to regain what it had lost in World War I, in 1939 Germany started World War II.

Painting of Lenin in the Russian village of Gorky in 1921

The Founding of the Soviet Union: 1922

For 300 years, the Romanov dynasty ruled Russia with absolute power. Romanov rule ended in 1917. After a revolution and three years of civil war, the Soviet Union was founded.

In the early 1900s, Russia was one of the poorest countries in Europe. In 1905, angry workers went on strike, crippling the country. In response, **Czar** Nicholas II created a **parliament** to pass reforms, but he refused to give the body any real power.

In 1914, Russia entered World War I to aid Serbia and its allies. The war proved disastrous. The number of Russian casualties was enormous. Food and fuel shortages plagued the economy. In the winter of 1917, women marched in the streets chanting one word: "Bread." Factory workers went on strike. Soldiers called in to quash the demonstrations joined the demonstrators instead. In March, Czar Nicholas was forced to give up power.

Wealthier members of parliament formed a temporary government. They shared power with councils—called

Vladimir Ilyich Ulyanov, better known as Lenin, was a Russian revolutionary who founded the Bolshevik Party. After Czar Nicholas gave up power, Lenin thought the men who took over the government were too **moderate.** He organized factory workers, peasants, and soldiers into the Red Army and seized control from the moderates on November 7, 1917. Lenin led the Soviet Union's new communist government until his death on January 21, 1924.

"soviets"—that had the support of peasants and factory workers. The most radical group in the soviets was the Bolshevik Party. Bolsheviks supported communism, an economic system in which the government distributes society's wealth evenly among citizens and all property is owned by the public, not by private citizens or businesses.

In November, the Bolsheviks seized control and established a new government with Vladimir Lenin as chairman. But by the spring of 1918, opposition to Bolshevik rule had risen. Supporters of the monarchy formed the White Army. Those fighting for the Bolshevik government were called the Red Army. Civil war raged until 1922 when the White Army was defeated.

Lenin divided Russia into a **confederation** of four republics. The country was renamed the Union of Soviet Socialist Republics (USSR), or the Soviet Union. Communists controlled all levels of government.

With the founding of the USSR, communism began to spread around the world. The Soviet Union became a world power and would go head-to-head with the United States for much of the 20th century.

THE DISCOVERY OF KING TUT'S TOMB

On November 26, 1922, British archaeologist Howard Carter discovered the tomb of the pharaoh Tutankhamen buried in the Valley of the Kings in Egypt. The teenage king had been mummified 3,000 years earlier. More than 5,000 objects were crammed into his tomb. This discovery inspired fashion designs in the 1920s.

Philo Farnsworth

The First Television: 1926

On January 26, 1926, Scottish inventor John Logie Baird gave the first public demonstration of a television. Before an audience of scientists and inventors, he broadcast images of two ventriloquist dummies.

Many inventors ridiculed Baird's television, which was a mechanical technology and produced only flickering images. This problem was solved by an American inventor named Philo Farnsworth.

Farnsworth grew up on a Utah farm without electricity or a telephone. By age six, he announced that he would be an inventor when he grew up. He taught himself physics and repaired radios. At age 14, while

Some people argue that American Charles Francis Jenkins invented the first television. He called his device a "radiovision." It used radio receivers to broadcast moving pictures on a small mirror. Jenkins showed the machine to the public on June 23, 1925. However, he did not broadcast moving pictures on it until a few months after John Logie Baird. In 1928, Jenkins formed the United States' first television station.

plowing a field, Farnsworth dreamed up the idea for an improved television. He envisioned an electronic system that would capture, transmit, and reproduce a clear moving picture.

Farnsworth became obsessed with the idea. After getting financial backing, he set up a makeshift lab in his living room. In 1928, Farnsworth demonstrated a working model of his television for reporters. By the late 1930s, electronic televisions were being produced and sold commercially. By the mid-1950s, color televisions were standard.

At first, people did not rush to buy televisions because there was little to watch. In the United States in 1946, only 6,000 people owned televisions. But in 1947, commercial television programming began. By 1951, some 12 million Americans owned televisions and tuned in to watch shows like *Howdy Doody* and *Amos 'n' Andy*.

Television changed the world. Today, satellite technology lets broadcasters beam news and entertainment over mountains and across oceans. World leaders use television to rally supporters and denounce opponents. Because the United States developed the greatest number of television programs at the cheapest price, American entertainment and American commercials showed up in living rooms across the world. This way, American culture influenced global culture.

RECORD-BREAKING SWIM

The same year as the first television broadcast, American Olympic champion Gertrude Ederle became the first woman to swim across the English Channel. Five men had already swum the channel, the fastest in 16 hours and 33 minutes. On August 6, 1926, Ederle beat that record, swimming from France to England in 14 hours and 31 minutes.

Chinese soldiers in Manchuria in 1931

The Chinese Civil War: 1927 to 1949

In 1927, a civil war tore China apart. The war lasted until 1949, changing the country and the world.

After a revolution in 1912 ended centuries of **imperial** rule in China, the country was not unified. Chiang Kai Shek led the Chinese National People's Party, which advocated **nationalism**, **capitalism**, and democracy. Mao Zedong led the Chinese Communist Party.

In 1927, disputes between the nationalists and communists erupted into civil war. Eventually, nationalist armies encircled the communist Red Army in southern China. The communist defeat seemed inevitable. But then in October 1934, the Red Army broke through the nationalist line, and Mao led 85,000 troops into northern China. Known as the Long March, the journey covered more than 4,000 miles and crossed 24 rivers and 18 mountain ranges.

When Japan invaded China in 1937, the nationalists and communists agreed to an uneasy truce. World War II ended in 1945 with Japan's defeat, but peace for the Chinese was short-lived. In the summer of 1946, Chiang ordered his armies into northern China to crush the communists' stronghold. By this time, the two sides had powerful allies. The United States provided the nationalists with weapons and aid, and the Soviet Union supported the communists.

MEET MAO ZEDONG

Mao Zedong served as chairman of the Chinese Communist Party until his death in 1976. In 1958, he launched the "Great Leap Forward," a plan to improve agriculture and manufacturing. It was a disaster. Between 35 million and 55 million people died from starvation, execution, and forced labor. In 1966, Mao launched the "Cultural Revolution." This campaign to revive people's revolutionary spirit and purge political opponents killed another 1.5 million people.

In late 1948, the communist army won a series of battles along the Yangtze River. This spelled the end for the nationalists. On October 1, 1949, Mao proclaimed the People's Republic of China and established the national capital in Beijing. Chiang fled to the island of Taiwan, claiming he was still president of China. But Mao declared that Taiwan was part of the People's Republic of China, too.

The two sides never signed a formal peace treaty to end this civil war. The conflict over Taiwan remains unresolved to this day. With the communist victory, the worldwide balance of power shifted. Western democracies feared that communism was spreading, and a global **arms race** began.

THE *SPIRIT OF ST. LOUIS*

On May 20, 1927, Charles Lindbergh took off from Long Island, New York, in a plane called the *Spirit of St. Louis*. After fighting fog, ice, and fatigue, Lindbergh landed in France on May 21. He had flown 3,610 miles in 33.5 hours and was the first person to fly solo and nonstop across the Atlantic.

Line outside a soup kitchen during the Great Depression

The Great Depression:
1929 to the 1930s

On October 29, 1929, the United States stock market crashed. This triggered the Great Depression, the worst economic collapse in modern history.

The United States economy had been slowing since the mid-1920s. The richest one percent of Americans owned most of the nation's wealth. Also, banks loaned money to people who gambled recklessly in the stock market. When stock prices fell, investors could not repay their loans. Banks collapsed, and people's savings disappeared overnight. Consumers stopped buying products, so businesses laid off workers.

MEET THE BONUS ARMY

At the height of the Great Depression in June 1932, 17,000 unemployed World War I **veterans** calling themselves the Bonus Army marched on Washington, DC, to request financial help from the government. President Hoover refused their request and sent in the US Army with tear gas and bayonets to clear them from DC. The veterans returned home, still penniless and jobless. Americans were outraged by this treatment of veterans. Hoover's handling of the Bonus Army contributed to his loss of the presidency and the election of Franklin Roosevelt that fall.

By 1932, 25 percent of working-age Americans could not find jobs.

To make matters worse, a drought struck the United States in 1931. This dry spell lasted eight years. Dry winds turned America's farmland into a dust bowl. Thousands of farmers migrated west, hoping to find work. Suicide and alcoholism rates spiked.

The Great Depression went global. International trade plunged by more than 50 percent. By 1932, 30 million people around the world, almost one in four, were unemployed.

Some countries responded with political **extremism**. In 1930, when Argentinian workers protested their lack of pay, the military seized control of the government. In Germany, Italy, and Japan, **fascist** governments rose to power on their promises to restore economic growth. These leaders solved their unemployment problem by giving people jobs as soldiers and in military industries.

Other nations tried to weave an economic safety net for their citizens. United States President Franklin Roosevelt created the New Deal. This program established **pensions** for retired workers, insured bank deposits, and regulated the stock market. Unemployment compensation laws protected people who lost their jobs.

Most of the world emerged from the Great Depression by the mid-1930s. However, the American economy did not recover until the country entered World War II in 1941.

WHEELBARROWS FULL OF MONEY

In 1923, Germany experienced extreme **inflation** when costs rose at dizzying rates. A wheelbarrow full of cash could barely buy a newspaper. By November 1923, one United States dollar was worth one trillion German marks.

Gandhi's Salt March

The Salt March: 1930

In the spring of 1930, Indian activist Mohandas Gandhi broke the law by making salt. In doing so, he started a movement that led to Indian independence.

Ever since the British took control of India in 1757, they had exploited India's resources and people. For example, Indians were required to buy heavily taxed salt from the British government, even though they could easily make their own.

Indian people had been divided since the early 1900s. Hindus and Muslims—the two main religions in India—fought, and social classes were strictly separated. But all Indians used salt. So Gandhi saw this as an issue that could unite people across the country. He believed that masses of people peacefully disobeying unfair laws could change society.

On March 12, 1930, the Salt March began with Gandhi and 79 followers. Their plan was to trek 240 miles to the coastal town of Dandi. Along the way, Gandhi addressed large crowds. By the time he reached the sea on April 5, tens of thousands had joined the march.

Upon reaching the salt flats on the beach, Gandhi picked up a small lump of salt crystal from the mud and said, "With this salt I am shaking the foundations of the British empire." With this action, Gandhi had

broken British law and sparked a movement. Millions of people across the country began producing their own salt.

The British gradually gave Indians more rights, but they clung to power until after World War II. Finally, at midnight on August 15, 1947, British rule in India ended.

British authorities partitioned India into two independent countries. India would be for Hindus and the new nation of Pakistan for Muslims. Gandhi hoped this solution would lead to a peaceful future for Indians. He did not live long enough to find out. Six months after independence, Gandhi was assassinated by a religious **fanatic**. However, his philosophy of civil resistance still inspires activists around the world who use Gandhi's methods to spark change.

THE FIRST WORLD CUP

After officials decided to drop soccer from the 1932 Olympic Games, soccer's international governing body organized its own world tournament, which is held every four years to this day. In July 1930, the first World Cup was held in Montevideo, Uruguay, before 93,000 spectators.

Adolf Hitler and crowd in the 1930s

The Rise of Nazism: 1933

In the 1920s, Germany's economy was in shambles, with high unemployment and skyrocketing inflation. Germans blamed their struggles on the harsh Treaty of Versailles that ended World War I.

Adolf Hitler was a veteran of that war. In 1919, he joined the National Socialist German Workers' Party, known as the Nazis. A charismatic speaker, Hitler soon became the party's leader. The Nazis believed in nationalism, global expansion, and racial purity. Nazis were anti-Semitic, meaning they hated Jewish people. Hitler believed Jews were racially inferior and blamed them for Germany's defeat in World War I.

MEET THE WHITE ROSE RESISTERS

Teenagers Hans and Sophie Scholl hated what the Nazis were doing to Germany. So the siblings and some friends organized a secret resistance movement called the White Rose. Between 1942 and 1943, they wrote, published, and distributed leaflets calling on Germans to rise up. The leaflets spread across Germany and Austria. On February 18, 1943, the Scholls were caught. Five days later, they were executed by guillotine. Hans Scholl's final words were: "Long live freedom!"

When the Great Depression began in 1929, the ranks of the Nazi Party swelled. Germans were drawn to Hitler's speeches. He blamed Jews and communists for the depression and promised to restore German pride.

After the 1932 elections, Hitler became chancellor of Germany. Once in power, he quickly changed the laws to give himself full authority. Freedom of speech and the press were banned. Political opponents were arrested and sent to **concentration camps**. Jewish people were similarly targeted. In 1935, the Nuremberg Laws stripped Jews of their German citizenship, barred them from many jobs, expelled them from school, and outlawed marriages between Jews and non-Jews.

In 1938, Hitler began to expand Germany's borders. He **annexed** Austria and then forced Czechoslovakia to surrender territory. Although this aggression alarmed Britain and France, they did not act. The death toll of World War I was still fresh in people's minds, and Hitler promised not to expand further.

Hitler broke this promise on September 1, 1939, when German forces invaded Poland. In response, Great Britain and France declared war on Germany. World War II had begun.

German armies quickly conquered much of Europe. Through starvation, forced labor, mass executions, and gas chambers, more than 6 million Jews and 5 million others were killed by the time World War II ended with Germany's defeat in 1945. This **genocide** is called the Holocaust.

NIGHT OF BROKEN GLASS

On the night of November 9, 1938, the sound of breaking glass shattered the air in cities throughout Germany. Gangs of Nazis rampaged through neighborhoods. That night 7,000 Jewish businesses were destroyed, 900 synagogues were burned, 91 Jews were killed, and 30,000 Jewish men were sent to concentration camps. The event is known as *Kristallnacht*, or the Night of Broken Glass.

CHAPTER THREE

1941
TO
1960

The aftermath of World War II cast a long
shadow over the 1940s and 1950s. The war
ended in 1945, but peace did not follow. Ideological differences and racial tensions ripped
countries apart in Asia, Africa, and Latin
America. The United States dropped two atomic
bombs on Japan in 1945, ushering in the Cold

War. This conflict between the United States and the Soviet Union impacted the world. When war erupted in Korea, Cuba, and Vietnam between communists and non-communists, the two superpowers backed opposing sides.

The Cold War was not confined to the battlefield. After the Soviet Union launched the first satellite into Earth's orbit in 1957, the space race began. The United States and the USSR poured money into space science. Both nations wanted to be the first to put a person on the moon.

While the Cold War played out in space, racial tensions tore South Africa apart. White South Africans controlled the government, and they developed a system of strict racial segregation called apartheid. Black South Africans faced daily discrimination. They fought back, first nonviolently and then with armed resistance.

In these conflict-riddled decades, there was one major success story. In 1945, world leaders founded the United Nations to foster friendly relations between countries. During the 1940s and 1950s, the United Nations helped resolve many conflicts.

Atomic bomb over Nagasaki

The Atomic Bomb: 1945

By the summer of 1945, World War II had ended in Europe, but Japan refused to surrender. So on August 6, a United States bomber dropped a new weapon over the city of Hiroshima. It was an atomic bomb. The explosion leveled five miles of city, killing 80,000 people instantly.

Still Japan did not surrender. A few days later, on August 9, the United States dropped a second atomic bomb on Nagasaki. About 40,000 people died at the moment of its impact. Finally, on August 15, the Japanese emperor surrendered. World War II was over.

Nazi Germany had initiated the research that led to the development of nuclear weapons. In 1939, scientists who had moved to the United States to escape Nazi brutality warned President Franklin Roosevelt that German physicists had successfully split a uranium atom. The United States was afraid the Nazis could use this knowledge to produce a bomb with huge destructive power. In an effort to make this discovery before Germany did, in 1941 Roosevelt launched the Manhattan Project, a top-secret research program to build an atomic bomb.

MEET J. ROBERT OPPENHEIMER

President Roosevelt appointed physicist J. Robert Oppenheimer to direct the Manhattan Project. After Oppenheimer witnessed the successful test of the world's first atomic bomb on July 16, 1945, he said, "We knew the world would not be the same." Oppenheimer saw the damage wrought by nuclear energy and he argued the United States should not develop bigger, deadlier weapons. Government officials accused him of being a "communist sympathizer," and Oppenheimer was blocked from further involvement in government science.

The world's first nuclear bomb was tested in the New Mexico desert at dawn on July 16, 1945. When the device exploded, the flash was visible for 200 miles. A mushroom cloud reached 40,000 feet into the sky, and a half-mile-wide crater opened in the earth.

As World War II ended, the world entered a nuclear age. By 1949, the Soviet Union had also developed an atomic bomb. The United States responded by building a hydrogen bomb with more firepower. The arms race had begun. This competition to have the largest and strongest military force in the world lasted for decades.

As of the early 21st century, nine countries possess approximately 9,000 nuclear weapons. No nation has used a nuclear bomb since the United States did on Japan in World War II. But as long as nuclear bombs exist, so does the threat they pose to the world.

THE BIKINI

On July 1, 1946, the United States tested an atomic bomb on the chain of Pacific islands called the Bikini Atoll. Two weeks later, French designer Louis Réard unveiled a two-piece women's swimsuit. He called it a bikini, claiming the suit would be as explosive as the US military tests had been.

United Nations meeting in 1945

The Founding of the United Nations: 1945

After World War II, world leaders were committed to resolving global conflicts in order to avoid future wars. On June 26, 1945, 50 nations signed the charter that created the United Nations.

Today, 193 countries are members of the United Nations. All members belong to the General Assembly, a policymaking body that meets annually to discuss important global issues.

The Security Council is the part of the United Nations responsible for maintaining world peace. The Council has five permanent members and 10 members

Vijaya Lakshmi Pandit used the United Nations to argue for Indian independence on a global stage. In 1945, this feminist politician traveled to San Francisco where the charter for the United Nations was being drafted. She gave interviews to the international press about why India deserved independence from Britain. In 1953, Pandit was elected the first woman president of the United Nations General Assembly.

that serve two-year terms. The Security Council can punish countries economically or authorize the use of force.

The Security Council has helped stabilize conflicts. For example, the Council helped prevent illegal weapons smuggling in Lebanon in the 1950s, supervised a cease-fire between India and Pakistan in 1965, and deescalated tensions between Israel and Syria in 1974.

However, Council members do not always cooperate. When civil war broke out in Rwanda in 1994, most members wanted to send international troops in to restore peace. However, the United States and France refused. So the United Nations was powerless to intervene as 800,000 Rwandans died in an ethnic genocide.

Other branches of the UN aid people around the world in different ways. When an earthquake killed 12,000 people in Iran in 1962, the UN's World Food Programme delivered tons of food to survivors. When war in Bangladesh sent people fleeing to neighboring India in 1971, the UN Refugee Agency provided humanitarian assistance to 10 million refugees. In 1992, the UN held the Earth Summit in Brazil, in which 154 nations agreed to reduce the pollution that causes climate change. Throughout the 1990s, the UN observed, supervised, or conducted elections in places ranging from Cambodia to the Democratic Republic of the Congo. The UN's World Health Organization helped eliminate smallpox, reduce HIV, and combat malaria, and the International Court of Justice settles disputes brought by member states. The United Nations continues to play a vital role in securing global peace and prosperity.

THE UNIVERSAL DECLARATION OF HUMAN RIGHTS

On December 10, 1948, world nations approved a list of rights every human deserves. The Universal Declaration of Human Rights begins, "All human beings are born free and equal in dignity and rights." The declaration called for an end to discrimination based on race, sex, religion, and national origin.

A Cold War bunker in Poland

The Cold War: 1947 to 1991

As soon as World War II ended, the Cold War began. In a cold war, nations use spies, threats, and economic **sanctions** instead of weapons to fight each other. From 1947 to 1989, the United States and the Soviet Union battled for global power.

The roots of the Cold War lay in philosophical differences. The United States is a capitalist country. The Soviet Union is a communist country. The United States believed communism threatened people's political and economic freedoms, whereas the Soviet Union believed capitalism exploited working people. Each nation was determined to spread its beliefs.

In 1947, the United States developed a two-part strategy for battling Soviet influence: containment and the Truman Doctrine. Containment focused on preventing the spread of communism. The Truman Doctrine was the United States' policy to give military and economic aid to people or countries threatened by communism anywhere in the world.

In 1949, two events spiked tensions. In August, the Soviet Union tested a nuclear bomb, escalating the arms race. Then on October 1, communists won the Chinese Civil War and founded the People's Republic of China.

MEET HO CHI MINH

Ho Chi Minh was a Vietnamese communist and nationalist. In 1941, he organized the Viet Minh, a group fighting for Vietnamese independence. First, Ho battled the Japanese army that occupied Vietnam during World War II. He then fought French colonial powers. After France's defeat in 1954, Vietnam was split into a communist north and a non-communist south. Determined to see Vietnam unified, Ho backed communists fighting against the South Vietnamese government. He served as president of North Vietnam until his death in 1969.

In 1950, the Cold War turned hot in Korea. When Japanese forces in Korea surrendered at the end of World War II, the country was divided, and two governments emerged. On June 25, 1950, the Soviet-backed regime in North Korea invaded the south. The United Nations authorized international troops to aid South Korea. A cease-fire was signed on July 27, 1953, but Korea remains divided into two countries today.

The Cold War also played out in the former French colony of Vietnam. When French rule crumbled in 1954, United States President Dwight Eisenhower sent military aid and advisers to the south, and the Soviets aided the north. By the early 1960s, the United States was bogged down in a costly and deadly civil war in Vietnam.

THE VOYAGE OF THE *KON-TIKI*

On April 28, 1947, Norwegian adventurer Thor Heyerdahl launched the raft *Kon-Tiki* from Peru to test his theory that ancient Americans settled Polynesia. Built from logs and rope, the *Kon-Tiki* was powered only by a sail. On August 7, the raft landed near Tahiti. Its journey of 4,300 miles proved an ancient voyage was possible.

Nelson Mandela, left, and Kweisi Mfume

Apartheid in South Africa: 1950 to 1994

White supremacy in South Africa was rooted in the country's history. In 1948, the white-controlled government cemented racism into law in a system called apartheid.

Jobs were posted for "whites only." Interracial marriages were outlawed. The Group Areas Act of 1950 created "homelands" for Black people in remote rural regions while the cities and best farmland were reserved for white people. The government stripped Black citizens of their South African citizenship. The police brutally enforced apartheid. For 50 years,

Desmond Tutu is a South African human rights activist. In 1975, he became the first Black Anglican Archbishop of Johannesburg, and he used this position to speak out against apartheid. Tutu led protests, supported national strikes, and pressured the United Nations to punish the South African government until it ended apartheid. Conflicts between police and protesters were frequent in South Africa in the 1980s. Tutu helped mediate these disputes. In 1984, he was awarded the Nobel Peace Prize.

hundreds of thousands of Black South Africans were arrested, kidnapped, or killed.

Black activists challenged apartheid from the start. In the 1950s, the African National Congress (ANC) organized boycotts, demonstrations, and strikes. The government arrested protesters and banned the ANC. So the group went underground, and in 1961, they created an armed wing of the party called the MK. Activist Nelson Mandela commanded the MK, which carried out 200 attacks on government facilities. But in 1963, Mandela and other MK operators were caught. Mandela was sentenced to life in prison.

Faced with this setback, the ANC turned to the international community for help. South Africa was banned from the Olympic Games. The United Nations expelled the country. European and American consumers pressured corporations to withdraw their investments in South Africa.

Economic pressure slowly worked. In 1990, South African President F.W. de Klerk lifted the ban on the ANC and released Nelson Mandela from prison. In 1993, lawmakers wrote a new constitution that guaranteed voting rights for all South Africans. When free elections were held in 1994, the ANC won control of parliament and Mandela was elected president. Apartheid was dead. But it would take decades to dismantle and overcome a history of **systemic racism**.

OLYMPIC BOYCOTT

Twenty-eight African countries boycotted the 1976 Summer Olympics in Montreal. These nations were angry because the International Olympic Committee had not banned New Zealand from the games. Earlier that year, New Zealand's rugby team played a tour in South Africa, violating the UN sports embargo against South Africa. The Olympic boycott generated international awareness for the anti-apartheid movement.

Sputnik satellite in orbit

The Space Race:
1957 to 1975

In the 1950s, outer space became the new battlefield in the Cold War. On October 4, 1957, the Soviets
launched *Sputnik*. This artificial satellite was the first
human-made object to orbit Earth. The United States
realized the possibilities and dangers of this technology and was determined to catch up to the Soviet
Union. The space race had begun.

In 1958, the United States launched its first satellite,
Explorer I. President Dwight Eisenhower also created
the National Aeronautics and Space Administration
(NASA), a federal agency dedicated to space exploration.

But in 1961, the Soviets proved they still held the lead. In April, Soviet cosmonaut Yuri Gagarin became the first person to orbit Earth. For one hour and 48 minutes, Gagarin circled the planet in *Vostok 1*. This huge victory for the Soviets was a crushing blow for NASA scientists. The next month, American astronaut Alan Shepard became the first American in space, but he flew for only 15 minutes.

MEET VALENTINA TERESHKOVA

On June 16, 1963, 26-year-old Valentina Tereshkova from the Soviet Union became the first woman to go into space. During her three-day mission, Tereshkova orbited the Earth 48 times. However, following her flight, the Soviets scrapped their women cosmonauts program. Another Soviet woman would not enter space until 1982. The first American woman to orbit Earth would be Sally Ride in 1983.

On May 25, 1961, United States President John F. Kennedy gave a speech before the United States Congress, vowing that Americans would land a man on the moon by the end of the decade.

Kennedy kept his promise. On July 20, 1969, half a billion people watched the lunar landing. As American astronaut Neil Armstrong took his first steps on the moon, he proclaimed, "That's one small step for man, one giant leap for mankind." The United States had won the space race.

Both the United States and the Soviet Union continued space exploration, but over time, collaboration became more important than competition. In 1975, American astronauts aboard an *Apollo* spacecraft docked in orbit beside a Soviet spacecraft. The two crews shared meals and conducted joint experiments. Construction on the International Space Station began in 1998. Since then, astronauts from 18 nations have spent time on the space station, cooperating on research projects and exploring ways to help humans travel to Mars and back safely.

ANIMALS IN SPACE

Before humans went into space, scientists tested space travel on animals. On November 3, 1957, the Soviets sent a dog named Laika into orbit aboard *Sputnik 2*. She died after a few hours. Over the years, monkeys, chimpanzees, dogs, squirrels, cats, rabbits, mice, rats, and fruit flies have all been rocketed into outer space in the name of science.

Fidel Castro with fellow revolutionary rebels in Cuba in 1959

Castro in Cuba: 1959

In 1959, a young Cuban named Fidel Castro and a band of revolutionaries overthrew the dictator of Cuba and established a communist government. Cuba is only 90 miles off the coast of Florida, so the United States' concern over communism skyrocketed.

Cuba had long been exploited by American corporations. To change that, Castro seized Cuban land owned by foreign businesses and put it under government control. Then he opened trade and diplomatic relations with the Soviet Union. Wealthy Cubans who owned corporations or plantations left the island for the United States.

On April 17, 1961, Cubans living in the United States invaded Cuba. Known as the Bay of Pigs invasion, the attack failed to topple Castro. The United States followed up by banning all trade with Cuba.

Castro and Soviet Premier Nikita Khrushchev decided to put nuclear missiles on Cuba in case the United States invaded again. An American spy plane spotted the construction site before the nuclear warheads had been delivered to the island. United States President John F. Kennedy demanded Khrushchev scrap the plan. Khrushchev refused.

For 13 days, the world watched as Soviet ships carrying nuclear missiles steamed toward Cuba. The US Navy circled the island, ready to stop the Soviets from landing. At the last minute, Khrushchev backed down. The United States promised not to invade Cuba again, and the Soviets sent their missiles home. The world breathed a sigh of relief.

From 1959 to 2011, Castro ruled Cuba with an iron fist in a silk glove. Literacy rates rose to 98 percent, and Cubans received free health care. But in return, they gave up some freedoms. Anyone who opposed Castro was jailed, or worse.

During his reign, Castro promoted communist revolutions in Asia, Africa, and Latin America. However, everything changed when the Soviet Union collapsed in 1991. Without Soviet assistance, unemployment and inflation skyrocketed. Castro had to ease government control over the economy. Travel and trade restrictions with the United States loosened a little by the early 21st century. Though Castro died in 2016, Cuba remains a communist country.

MARIEL BOATLIFT

In April 1980, Fidel Castro announced that anyone who wanted to leave Cuba could do so. Some 125,000 Cubans fled to the United States on boats and rafts. This included thousands of inmates of prisons and mental institutions whom Castro had ordered released.

CHAPTER FOUR

1961

TO

1980

The competing themes of division and unity marked major events in the 1960s and 1970s.

In 1961, ideological divisions prompted the East German government to build a wall around West Berlin. East Germany's communist government wanted to isolate its citizens from Western influences.

Differences in beliefs were also behind the Cultural Revolution in China. Leader Mao Zedong resisted any changes to his version of communism. Millions of Chinese were sent to "re-education camps" to brainwash them into accepting Mao's view of the world.

Religious intolerance separated Catholics and Protestants in Northern Ireland. When the Catholic **minority** demonstrated for equality and independence, the Protestant majority resisted. Thirty years of conflict followed.

But this era was also a time when people united behind common causes. The rock band the Beatles took the world by storm in the early 1960s and helped launch a counterculture. Young people connected by similar passions challenged traditional ways of thinking and behaving. The Organization of African Unity formed, so newly independent African nations could cooperate to solve common problems. And after decades of conflict, Israel and Egypt closed out this era by finally signing a joint peace treaty.

People in West Berlin peer over the Berlin Wall, 1960s

The Berlin Wall: 1961

On August 13, 1961, citizens of Berlin, Germany, woke up to a changed world. Overnight, a barbed-wire barrier appeared along the 28-mile border between the east and west sides of the city. Within a few months, the barbed wire became a 13-foot concrete wall. Watchtowers loomed over the border, and East German soldiers guarded checkpoints. No one could cross without official approval. Parents were cut off from children and husbands separated from wives. The Berlin Wall was the most physical symbol of the Cold War.

When Germany was defeated in World War II, the Allies divided the country into four occupation zones.

Germany's capital city, Berlin, was divided, too. This split was supposed to be temporary. But as Cold War tensions hardened, Germany became two separate countries. West Germany was democratic and capitalist, whereas East Germany was **totalitarian** and communist. Berlin was also divided into a free West Berlin and communist East Berlin.

MEET JOHN F. KENNEDY

On June 26, 1963, United States President John F. Kennedy spoke before 120,000 West Berliners. He did not threaten or rant. Instead, Kennedy urged Soviets and Americans to view each other with open minds rather than through blinders shaded by fear. Kennedy's words bore fruit. Two months later, the United States and the Soviet Union signed a treaty to limit the testing of nuclear weapons.

While the West German economy prospered, East Germany's collapsed. So citizens of East Germany abandoned their country by walking across the border separating East and West Berlin. By 1961, three million of East Germany's most educated citizens had moved west. That's why East German and Soviet authorities decided to plug this leak by building a wall around West Berlin.

The Berlin Wall was a flash point in the Cold War. In October 1961, a crisis over an American diplomat who crossed into East Berlin escalated. The American military commander in West Berlin sent 10 tanks to Checkpoint Charlie, the most used crossing point between East and West Berlin. Alarmed, the Soviets ordered 10 Russian tanks to the border, too. The confrontation lasted 16 hours as the opposing tanks stood only 100 yards apart. But neither American President John F. Kennedy nor Soviet Premier Nikita Khrushchev thought Berlin was worth a nuclear war. Both sides withdrew. The Berlin Wall remained in place for almost 30 years, a visual reminder of the divisions between the capitalist West and communist East.

DEATH ON THE WALL

On August 17, 1961, 18-year-old Peter Fechter was shot by East German guards while trying to escape over the Berlin Wall. He collapsed on the East German side. Guards refused to let anyone help him. Fechter lay dying for almost one hour. During the years the Berlin Wall stood, more than 262 people died trying to cross to freedom in the West.

Ugandan President Idi Amin Dada, left, and Congolese President Marien Ngouabi

The Organization of African Unity: 1963

In 1963, 32 newly independent African nations met in Ethiopia and formed the Organization of African Unity (OAU). They wanted to achieve strength through cooperation.

After World War II, the hold European nations had on their African colonies began to crumble. In 1957, Ghana was the first African country to gain independence. Ghanaians achieved this with a campaign of boycotts and national strikes.

Civil rights activists were using similar civil disobedience strategies in the United States.

Kwame Nkrumah was born in the Gold Coast, a British colony in West Africa. He attended college in the United States, where he saw alternatives to the British way of governing. Nkrumah returned to the Gold Coast in 1949, formed the Convention Peoples Party, and led a movement that achieved independence in 1957. The Gold Coast became the Republic of Ghana. Nkrumah was elected prime minister and president. Ghana's route to independence became the model for the rest of Africa.

Africans and Black Americans were linked by the philosophy of Pan-Africanism. This belief that people of African descent have common interests developed in the United States in the late 19th century.

1960 was called the Year of Africa because 17 nations gained independence from Europe that year. The OAU was formed to define the relationship these nations would have with one another and the world. Eventually, 54 of Africa's 55 countries would join the OAU.

Member nations were determined to eliminate colonialism throughout the continent, and the group financed independence movements in countries still controlled by Europe. The OAU's greatest success was in providing support to independence movements in other African countries. Most of the continent was free by the mid-1970s. The OAU also helped negotiate treaties among member countries over issues like refugee status and human rights. However, the OAU was unable to bring peace, prosperity, and stability to all of Africa. Members had agreed that they would not interfere in each other's domestic affairs. So the organization did not confront brutal dictatorships in Uganda or intervene to prevent the Rwandan Genocide.

OAU members decided their organization could not meet the demands of the new millennium. So on July 9, 2002, the OAU was replaced with the African Union. This group's goal is to create a cooperative, peaceful, and prosperous Africa.

CELEBRATION OF BLACK CULTURE

In April 1966, the first World Festival of Negro Arts was launched in Dakar, Senegal. More than 2,000 Black participants celebrated the creativity of a vibrant global Black culture.

The Beatles in 1963

The Rise of the Beatles: 1960s

In 1961, a band made up of four teenagers from Liverpool, England, produced their first record. John Lennon, Paul McCartney, George Harrison, and Ringo Starr were the Beatles. Their band launched a musical revolution that became the soundtrack to the 1960s counterculture—a global movement in which young people rejected the attitudes, values, and behaviors of their parents' generation.

On February 9, 1964, 73 million Americans watched the band perform on TV on *The Ed Sullivan Show*. Over the next few years, the Beatles made albums and movies and played concerts all over the world.

As the Beatles' music evolved, so did the culture of their fans. In the United States, the civil rights movement had already exposed cracks in the idea of American progress. Then in the 1960s, America became involved in the Vietnam War. As the war escalated, opposition among young people grew. A counterculture emerged along two tracks: Some youth fought injustice whereas others rejected society altogether.

The fighters made up the New Left, a loose coalition of youth-led organizations on college campuses in the United States and Europe. Some groups protested

the Vietnam War while others marched for equal rights for all. In 1968, a massive student strike in Paris almost brought down the French government, and long-haired youth staged a failed uprising in communist Czechoslovakia.

Those who chose to drop out of society entirely were called Hippies. They wanted to create a society based on peace, love, and pleasure. Hippies dressed in tie-dye and bell bottoms. They lived in communal houses, made their own laws, and shared their wealth.

The counterculture disappeared by the 1970s, but it left a legacy. The protests of the era addressed taboo topics such as racism, sexism, and homophobia. Many Western nations passed laws protecting the civil rights of minorities. The Beatles broke up in 1969, but their songs became classics that are still popular today.

AN EXPERIMENTAL ALBUM

Released in 1967, the Beatles' album *Sgt. Pepper's Lonely Hearts Club Band* mirrored the mood of global youth with songs about drugs, expanding the mind, and dropping out of society. *Sgt. Pepper* showed that the Beatles were redefining themselves. This gave their fans the permission to do the same.

Chinese Red Guards during the Cultural Revolution

The Chinese Cultural Revolution: 1966

The Cultural Revolution began in China in 1966. It lasted a decade and left a devastating legacy.

In the 1960s, Chinese Communist Party leader Mao Zedong wanted to revive China's revolutionary spirit and weed out his opponents. So he launched the Great Proletarian Cultural Revolution in August of 1966. Mao called on the nation to rid society of "the four olds": "old culture, old customs, old habits, and old beliefs." After accusing educators of polluting students' minds with capitalist ideas, he closed all schools.

When the Cultural Revolution began, Xi Jinping was the outcast son of a disgraced official. The Red Guard bullied Xi and his siblings so badly that one sister died by suicide. Xi was sent to the countryside for "re-education." For six years, he labored in the fields and slept in a cave. But instead of rejecting communism, Xi embraced it. When the Cultural Revolution ended, he climbed the ranks of the Communist Party. In 2013, Xi Jinping became president of China.

Party officials encouraged youth to turn in anyone they suspected of being a capitalist. When schools opened up again, Chinese students set up divisions of a militant youth movement called the Red Guard on campuses across the country. Teachers, principals, and college professors were forced to publicly confess their supposed crimes. Gangs of teens dressed in military uniforms and red armbands roamed city streets. They attacked anyone who looked middle class. In August and September of 1966, 1,772 people were killed in Beijing alone.

China was in chaos. Miners and factory workers left their jobs to battle rival groups. Because trains and trucks were used to move Red Guards around the country, the transportation of resources and products ground to a halt. As food disappeared from store shelves, hunger began to stalk city dwellers. Mao ordered millions of China's professionals and students sent to the countryside for "re-education." This schooling involved backbreaking farm work.

Mao's death in 1976 ended the Cultural Revolution, but it left behind a scarred nation. Over 1.5 million people were killed. Millions more were imprisoned or had their property seized by the state. Because universities were closed for a decade, there were few educated professionals to help China recover.

Mao had launched the Cultural Revolution to turn China into a model communist country, but it had the opposite effect. The Cultural Revolution caused people to lose faith in the system and paved the way for reforms in the 1980s that allowed capitalism into the Chinese economy.

THE GREAT FAMINE

Between 1959 and 1961, poor government policies in China led to three years of hunger known as the Great Famine. To survive, people ate things like tree bark, grass roots, mice, and soup made from lard and soy sauce. An estimated 45 million Chinese people starved to death.

People in the streets during Bloody Sunday

Bloody Sunday: 1972

In 1972, British soldiers fired into an unarmed crowd of civil rights demonstrators in Derry, Northern Ireland. Known as Bloody Sunday, this event sparked more violence in an already troubled region.

The roots of Bloody Sunday go back to the early 20th century. In 1919, the Irish Republican Army (IRA) rose up to throw off British rule in Ireland. After three years of fighting, the island was partitioned. The mostly Catholic southern counties became an independent Irish state. But the Protestant-dominated northern counties remained part of Britain.

Catholics who remained in Northern Ireland faced political, social, and economic discrimination. Catholics and Protestants lived in separate neighborhoods and attended separate schools. Most Catholics were nationalists who wanted to unify with the southern counties to form a single Irish Republic. Protestants, on the other hand, were unionists, meaning they wanted to remain part of Great Britain. In the early 1960s, the IRA and unionist **paramilitary** groups battled daily on city streets. In 1969, the British government sent troops to restore order.

The IRA became more aggressive, targeting the police and army. British soldiers shot first and asked

MEET THE PEACE PEOPLE

On August 10, 1976, British soldiers shot a fleeing IRA gunman in Belfast, Northern Ireland. The man's car swerved onto the pavement, killing three children. Betty Williams, one of the first on the scene, was horrified. She gathered thousands of signatures on a petition to end the violence. The dead children's aunt, Mairead Corrigan, joined Williams. Together they formed the Peace People movement, which included both Catholics and Protestants. The women organized marches and demonstrations calling for an end to the bloodshed.

questions later. This was the atmosphere that led to Bloody Sunday on January 30, 1972.

A crowd of 15,000 marched to protest a new bill that would permit police to hold people indefinitely without a trial. British authorities sent in troops to break up the demonstration. When some youth threw stones at the soldiers, the troops responded with rubber bullets, tear gas, and water cannons. Then they opened fire into the crowd. Thirteen people died and 17 were wounded. This was just one tragedy in an era known as the Troubles.

In 1998, the Good Friday Agreement determined that Northern Ireland would remain part of Great Britain, but that Catholics and Protestants would share power in the government. This compromise allowed for peace after 33 years of tumult and more than 3,000 deaths.

MUNICH MASSACRE

On September 5, 1972, eight Palestinian terrorists broke into the Olympic Village during the games in Munich, Germany. The terrorists killed two members of the Israeli team and held nine more as hostages. All hostages were killed during a failed rescue attempt, along with five terrorists and a German police officer. The Olympic Games resumed 24 hours later.

Egyptian President Anwar Sādāt, left, and Israeli Prime Minister Menachem Begin in 1978

Peace in the Middle East: 1978 to 1979

The roots of conflict in the Middle East go back to at least the early 20th century, and peace has proved hard to achieve.

After World War I, the British ruled the region of Palestine, which both Arabs and Jews called home. In 1947, the United Nations divided Palestine into separate Arab and Jewish states and made Jerusalem an international city, which meant it would not be under the control of any nation's government.

On May 14, 1948, Jews declared the territory an independent nation named Israel. Immediately,

United States President Jimmy Carter received the Nobel Peace Prize in 2002. Not only did Carter mediate the Camp David Accords, but he also continued to do humanitarian work after his presidency ended. Carter partnered with Habitat for Humanity to build housing for homeless people. He also served as an international election observer to foster democracy. The former president and his wife founded the Carter Center to fight disease and improve economic conditions around the world.

five neighboring Arab nations invaded Israel. The war ended in 1949. Israel won, taking 77 percent of the territory of Palestine and the city of Jerusalem. More than 700,000 Palestinians fled or were expelled from their homes.

In 1967, Israel started the Six-Day War and seized more of Palestine's land, as well as territory from neighboring Jordan and Egypt. Another half-million Palestinians had to flee their homes.

The United Nations passed a series of resolutions calling for the end of aggressions, for the return of lands gained in war, and for Palestinians to have the right to govern themselves. But peace negotiations between Israel and its Arab neighbors kept breaking down.

In 1978, United States President Jimmy Carter invited Egyptian President Anwar Sādāt and Israeli Prime Minister Menachem Begin to a peace summit at Camp David, the presidential retreat in Maryland.

From the outset, it was rough going. Every meeting ended in an argument. Sādāt and Begin refused to compromise. The summit was on the verge of breaking down, but President Carter did not give up.

Finally, after 23 drafts, the men agreed on a framework for peace. Egypt and Israel would establish diplomatic relations and Israel would withdraw from the Sinai Peninsula, which had belonged to Egypt. Sādāt and Begin formally signed the Egypt-Israel peace treaty on March 26, 1979. The men shared the 1978 Nobel Peace Prize for this historic achievement.

MASS SUICIDE AT JONESTOWN

After being accused of fraud and abuse in California, cult leader Jim Jones moved his Peoples Temple congregation to Guyana, South America. In a jungle settlement, Jones ordered his followers to drink poison. Those who refused were shot. More than 900 people, one-third of them children, died.

CHAPTER FIVE

1981

TO

2000

The last two decades of the 20th century were darkened by fear and failed revolutions. But hope remained as the Cold War came to a peaceful end and technological advancements created breakthroughs in science and communications.

A mysterious virus sparked global panic in the 1980s. Eventually, scientists identified the virus that causes AIDS and developed a treatment, but not until millions died in a global pandemic.

Others died from drought, civil war, and famine in Ethiopia. The world paid little attention until world musicians stepped up to organize global relief concerts.

During these two decades, democracy struggled to find a foothold in Zimbabwe. After gaining independence, democracy lay within its grasp. But when a ruler refused to relinquish power, this chance slipped away.

Democracy did expand in Eastern Europe. After massive peaceful protests, the Berlin Wall came down in 1989. Then communist governments across Eastern Europe fell one after another.

The 20th century closed with revolutions in communications and science. After a British scientist invented the World Wide Web, people could connect via the internet. In 2000, the Human Genome Project published the results of a decade-long effort to map every gene in the human body. Human knowledge seemed boundless.

AIDS Memorial Quilt in 1980

The HIV Epidemic: 1983

An unknown virus appeared in the United States in the early 1980s. Because only gay men were getting sick at first, and **LGBTQ** people were discriminated against, the condition was initially dismissed as a "gay plague." But by the end of the 20th century, the virus became a global pandemic.

In January 1981, doctors in Los Angeles were puzzled. Healthy young men were contracting a rare form of pneumonia only seen in people with damaged immune systems. All the patients were gay.

Then similar infections appeared in patients outside of Los Angeles, including in heterosexual people, recipients of blood transfusions, and people who used drugs.

In 1982, scientists named the illness acquired immunodeficiency syndrome, or AIDS. Cases were reported in Europe and Africa.

In 1983, a team of French researchers discovered AIDS was caused by the human immunodeficiency virus, or HIV. The virus is transmitted during sex without condoms, by sharing needles through drug use, and through blood transfusions,

the birthing process, and breast milk. Over time, HIV damages the immune system so it cannot fight off infection. When that happens, the person has AIDS.

Then scientists announced HIV could be passed through unprotected sex between any people and blood transfusions. AIDS became front-page news.

As the illness spread, so did fear and discrimination. People with HIV were banned from public restrooms. Cab drivers refused to give people rides. HIV-positive people were evicted from their apartments, fired from their jobs, and kicked out of school.

Education programs and improved drug therapies reduced the spread of HIV in the United States by two-thirds from 1985 to 2010. But the virus found fresh ground. By 2001, AIDS was the leading cause of death in Africa, and between 2010 and 2020, rates in Central Asia soared by 72 percent.

Treatment is the silver lining in the AIDS story. In 1996, scientists developed a drug regimen that transformed AIDS from a death sentence into a manageable lifelong illness.

AIDS MEMORIAL QUILT

The AIDS Memorial Quilt is one of the world's largest community art projects. When displayed in Washington, DC, in 1987, the quilt had 1,920 panels, each bearing the name of an AIDS victim. By 2020, there were 48,000 panels.

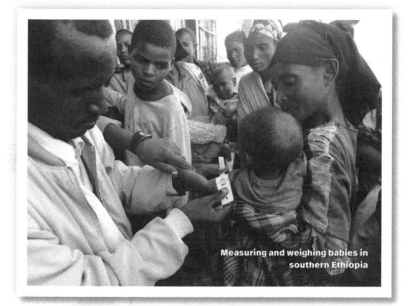

Measuring and weighing babies in southern Ethiopia

Famine in Ethiopia: 1983

Between 1983 and 1985, more than one million Ethiopians starved to death in one of the worst humanitarian crises of the 20th century.

Drought started Ethiopia's food shortage, but a 30-year civil war turned it into a crisis. Too little rain led to poor harvests in northern Ethiopia. There were also armed rebellions in the northern provinces of Tigray and Eritrea. In the spring of 1983, the Ethiopian army launched an offensive to quash the rebels. The army burned grain supplies, bombed fields, cut down orchards, and shot livestock. Soon people began to starve.

In March 1983, the Ethiopian government appealed for international aid. However, Cold War rivalries still existed, and Ethiopian President Mengistu Haile Mariam was supported by the Soviet Union. Western nations did not want to prop up the pro-communist government, so they held back aid.

Then on October 23, a televised news report from a refugee camp showed graphic footage of dead, starving, and diseased Ethiopians. The world finally paid attention.

Horrified by the crisis, British musician Bob Geldof organized a series of relief efforts. First, British and Irish pop artists recorded a single, raising $10 million for food aid. American musicians followed suit. Their single, "We Are the World," earned another $44 million for famine relief.

Still, politics prevented food from reaching those in need. The Ethiopian government set up refugee camps in the south to lure the hungry out of the rebelling regions. But when people reached camp, there was not enough food for everyone. Instead, the government was using food aid to pay soldiers fighting in Tigray and Eritrea.

Musical artists stepped up again. Bob Geldof organized the benefit concert Live Aid. On July 13, 1985, 75 musical acts performed in concerts in Philadelphia and London. One billion viewers watched on live television. Live Aid raised $127 million for famine relief.

The publicity around Live Aid spurred Western nations to send more grain to Ethiopia, and the famine ended. However, conflict, drought, and hunger continue to plague many African countries.

OPERATION MOSES

In the middle of the Ethiopian famine, Israel smuggled thousands of Ethiopian Jews out of refugee camps. Posing as businesspeople, Israeli secret agents snuck truckloads of Jews into a rented resort. Then agents transported the refugees to Israeli ships and planes. The smuggling operation stopped in 1985 when the story leaked to the press, but 8,000 Ethiopian Jews had already made it to Israel.

Robert Mugabe, George Silundika, and Joshua Nkomo

The Struggle for Democracy: 1980s

In the 1980s, struggles for equality and freedom arose on several continents. The example of the African nation of Zimbabwe illustrates how hard it is to build a long-lasting democracy.

From the 1880s until 1965, Zimbabwe was a British colony called Southern Rhodesia. During this colonial period, white people were a minority but they controlled the land, the economy, and the government. Black people labored in fields and mines, and they lived in poverty with no political rights. In 1962, Great Britain announced that Southern Rhodesia could have independence, but only if it recognized the rights of Black people. White people refused to accept this. They declared their independence without British permission, calling their nation Rhodesia. This sparked a 15-year war between the Rhodesian government and the Zimbabwe African People's Union (ZAPU).

MEET TANK MAN

On June 5, 1989, a man blocked a row of military tanks rolling through Tiananmen Square in Beijing, China. Hundreds of thousands of pro-democracy college students had been protesting in the square since April. The June 5 crackdown ended the protests. The Chinese government censored news of the event. No one knows the identity or fate of "tank man," but he became a symbol of the fight for freedom around the world.

After years of fighting, the Rhodesian government agreed to hold free elections. When ballots were cast in February 1980, ZAPU won a majority and Robert Mugabe became the first prime minister of the new nation called Zimbabwe. Black Zimbabweans finally had a voice in their own future.

But this democracy was short-lived. Not long after taking office, Mugabe began to eliminate his political opponents. Civilians suspected of hiding anyone who disagreed with Mugabe were targeted. By the 1990s, 20,000 people had been killed.

The government had promised to redistribute land more fairly but failed to do so. In 1997, Black people began to seize land from white farmers on their own. Protests and violence followed, and the Zimbabwean economy plummeted.

The hallmark of a democracy is free and fair elections. Mugabe was reelected multiple times, but these elections were tainted by his supporters beating and killing opponents. In 2008, Mugabe proclaimed, "Only God, who appointed me, will remove me." Ultimately, the military removed Mugabe in 2017. He died in 2019, but Zimbabwe still does not have a fully functioning democracy.

BRAZIL ENDS DICTATORSHIP

In 1964, Brazil's military ousted the democratically elected president, leading to more than 20 years of military dictatorship. Brazil's congress was dissolved. News was censored. Thousands of people were arrested and disappeared. Only after the economy crashed in the early 1980s did the Brazilians elect a civilian president once again.

People on the Berlin Wall.

The Fall of Communism:
1989 to 1991

Through the fall of 1989, communist governments in Eastern Europe fell like dominoes. This collapse destroyed the Berlin Wall, ended the Cold War, and splintered the Soviet Union.

The unraveling of communism began in Poland, when Polish voters elected a non-communist legislature. The world expected Soviet tanks to roll in and prevent the democratic government from taking power. This had happened in the past. But the new president of the USSR, Mikhail Gorbachev, refused to intervene in Poland.

Boris Yeltsin was the father of democracy in Russia. In 1990, Communist Party members selected Yeltsin to be president of Russia, the largest Soviet republic. Instead, Yeltsin quit the party and called for free elections. Yeltsin won, making him the first legitimately elected leader in Russia's 1,000 years of government. When the USSR broke up, Yeltsin served as president of Russia until 1999. He ended censorship and introduced reforms to allow businesses to compete more freely.

Democracy was contagious. After months of public demonstrations, Hungary's communist government transitioned to a democracy by October. Then East Germany followed suit. Tens of thousands of East Germans took to the streets. On November 9, East German leaders held a press conference. To reduce tensions, they promised to relax travel restrictions. But the official in charge of the press conference mangled the message his superiors had written. He made it sound as though the government had opened up the Berlin Wall.

People swarmed the border, chanting, "Open the gates!" East German guards had no orders. Should they fire on the crowds or open the gates? As the crowds reached dangerous levels, the supervisor at one check-point made a historic decision. He opened the wall.

Thousands of joyful people swept into West Berlin. Using hammers and picks, they knocked off chunks of the physical symbol of the Cold War.

On December 3, 1989, the United States and Soviet presidents issued a joint statement: The Cold War was over. By year's end, communist regimes were ousted in Czechoslovakia and Romania. In 1990, East and West Germany were united.

Demands for freedom spread to the Soviet repub lics next. One by one, they declared independence. On December 26, 1991, the Soviet Union was officially broken up into 15 separate countries. The world's oldest and most influential communist country was gone.

THE CHERNOBYL DISASTER

On April 26, 1986, a reactor at the Chernobyl nuclear power plant in the Soviet Union exploded. Nuclear fallout rained down on the nearby town of Pripyat, Ukraine, and blew on clouds across Europe. Thousands—if not hundreds of thousands—died from the contamination.

Tim Berners-Lee

The Invention of the World Wide Web: 1990

In the internet's early days, the only way to access information from someone else was to physically log on to their computer. This was cumbersome and time-consuming. Then British computer scientist Tim Berners-Lee came up with the idea of a global computer network.

When Berners-Lee was a software engineer at a research organization in Switzerland in the 1980s, he realized scientists could not easily share information stored on their computers. By October 1990, he had created three technologies to solve this problem, which together form the foundation of the World Wide Web.

First, computers use the same formatting language, HTML, to communicate on the web. Second is the Uniform Resource Locator, or URL. This is a system for recognizing the location of web pages. Finally, the HTTP, or Hypertext Transfer Protocol, is a method of "serving up" web pages on request.

Berners-Lee realized the web would only take off if he did not charge a fee for using it. So in 1993, he announced that the code to put a website on the internet would be free, forever. This development sparked a wave of creativity. In 1993, only 130 websites existed. By the following year, there were 2,700, and in 2020, 6 billion websites were available.

The World Wide Web transformed modern life. In 1994, the online shopping site Amazon was created, changing the way people buy products. In 1998, the search engine Google was introduced. It became such a basic tool that in 2006, the verb "googling" was added to dictionaries. Wikipedia, the online encyclopedia, was added in 2001. Facebook, YouTube, and Twitter let people interact without ever meeting in person.

Never before has it been so easy to get information, communicate with people, or start a business. The invention of the World Wide Web has been revolutionary.

ATTACK OF MAFIABOY

In 2000, 15-year-old Canadian hacker Michael Calce, known online as MafiaBoy, brought down some of the world's biggest websites. After Calce took over some university networks, he harnessed their computing power to attack Amazon, CNN, Dell, E*Trade, eBay, and Yahoo. The action was a wake-up call for companies to improve their internet security.

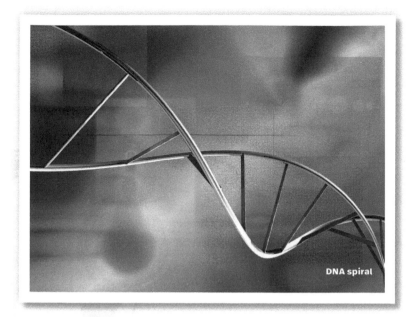

DNA spiral

The Human Genome Project: 1990 to 2000

In 1990, an international team of scientists began the Human Genome Project. Researchers dove into the immense task of mapping and understanding all the genes humans have in their bodies, known as the human genome.

The project took 13 years to complete and involved 1,700 researchers from the United States, Great Britain, France, Germany, Japan, and China.

Sequencing human genes is like putting together a complicated puzzle. First, scientists collect a sample such as saliva. Then they make many copies of the

The Human Genome Project's results were scheduled to be unveiled at the White House on June 26, 2000, but researchers didn't have a computer program that could sequence the 400,000 fragments of DNA that had been identified. James Kent, a graduate student in biology who had once been a computer programmer, offered to help. After working around the clock for four weeks, Kent successfully sequenced the human genome just four days before the public presentation.

DNA in the saliva and break these copies into smaller pieces. Finally, the scientists analyze the chemical reactions of each small piece to determine its sequence in the larger genome.

The results of the Human Genome Project were enlightening. Researchers found that humans have only 20,000 to 25,000 genes, fewer than rice or water fleas. This proves that the number of genes an organism has does not determine how complex it is.

Francis Collins, the director of the National Human Genome Research Institute, described the genome as a book that serves many purposes. Like a history book, the genome tells the story of the human species over time. Like a technical manual, the genome contains a detailed blueprint of every cell. Finally, like a medical textbook, the genome contains information to help treat, prevent, and cure diseases.

The legacy of the Human Genome Project is still being determined. Genetic testing has led to the development of groundbreaking new drugs to treat certain types of cancers. The project also spawned hundreds of businesses. Consumers can find companies that use genetics to trace people's ancestry, identify disease risk, and make diet recommendations. However, there is still much about the genome that scientists do not understand. Determining the biological function of every human gene will take decades, if not longer.

CLONING DOLLY THE SHEEP

On July 5, 1996, scientists in Scotland successfully cloned a sheep. They called the sheep Dolly. This development sparked controversy. Supporters argued cloning could lead to medical advancements that could treat diseases such as Alzheimer's and Parkinson's. Opponents insisted cloning technology is unsafe and unethical.

LOOKING AHEAD

At the start of the 20th century, Einstein's theory of relativity revealed truths about the vast universe. At the end of the century, the Human Genome Project revealed truths about microscopic human cells. In between, technology impacted life in areas from transportation and communication to health and warfare.

Conflict was another theme running through the 20th century. Competition for land and resources sparked World Wars I and II. A desire for independence led to the end of colonial regimes in India and Africa. Ideological differences erupted in revolutions around the world and gave birth to the Cold War.

But throughout the global chaos ran a constant thread of creativity and ingenuity. Television was invented. Humans landed on the moon. Music spurred the development of a counterculture and raised funds for famine victims.

The history of the 20th century serves as both hope and warning to citizens of the 21st century: Change is inevitable, but what form it takes remains to be seen. Will political change move nations toward democracy or dictatorship? Will economic change create prosperity or poverty? Will technology save humankind or be its doom? Fate will not determine the history of the 21st century, but people's choices will.

GLOSSARY

activist: A person who works for political or social change

alliance: A union between two or more parties over ideas or ideals

annex: To add a territory into a country or city

arms race: A competition between hostile nations to build up their weapons arsenals

boycott: To stop buying from a company or using its products as a form of peaceful protest

capitalism: An economic system in which private companies and individuals own all property

civil disobedience: Peacefully refusing to follow a law as a form of protest

communism: A system in which business, property, and goods are owned by the government

concentration camp: A place where a government imprisons groups of political dissenters or persecuted minorities

confederation: An alliance of nations working together toward a common goal

czar: An emperor of Russia before 1917

democratic republic: A form of government in which citizens elect leaders to represent them

dictator: A ruler with total control that is often used violently

element: A substance that cannot be broken down into any other substance

exile: A punishment in which a person is barred from living in their homeland

extremism: Radical political or religious views

fanatic: Someone who holds extreme political or religious views

fascism: A political philosophy marked by strong national pride and a ruler who holds absolute power

genocide: The deliberate killing of an entire racial, political, or cultural group

ideology: A set of beliefs

imperial: Relating to an empire or emperor

Indigenous: Someone who is native to an area

inflation: A rise in prices and fall in the value of money

Inuits: Indigenous people living in or originating from the Arctic areas of Canada, Alaska, and Greenland

LGBTQ: Acronym for lesbian, gay, bisexual, transgender, and queer/questioning

minority: A group of people who make up less than half of their society

moderates: People whose political views are in the middle; they do not favor extreme views or major change

nationalism: To put your nation's interests above others

pandemic: A disease that spreads across many countries

paramilitary: Similar to, but more unofficial than, an organized military

parliament: A lawmaking body of government

pension: Regular payment given to people by their former employer after they retire

reform: To improve something by changing current conditions or practices

sanctions: Economic penalties imposed to punish a foreign country or force it to obey international law

stock market: The exchange—through buying and selling—of shares in publicly traded companies

systemic racism: A system of policies and practices that exist throughout a society that treats people differently based on race

totalitarian: A political system in which those in power have complete control over citizens

treaty: A written agreement between countries

veterans: People who served in the military

white supremacy: The belief that white people are superior to people of color

RESOURCES

Books

Ellis, Deborah. *Three Wishes: Palestinian and Israeli Children Speak*. Toronto, Canada: Groundwood Books, 2004.

Hale, Nathan. *Treaties, Trenches, Mud, and Blood*. New York: Abrams, 2014.

McGinty, Alice B. *Gandhi: A March to the Sea*. New York: Two Lions Publishing, 2013.

Yue, Guo, and Clare Farrow. *Little Leap Forward: A Boy in Beijing*. Cambridge, MA: Barefoot Books, 2008.

Museums

The Museum of Flight (Seattle, Washington)

Smithsonian National Air and Space Museum (Washington, DC)

United States Holocaust Memorial Museum (Washington, DC)

Websites

History.com

PBS.org

USHMM.org

SELECTED REFERENCES

Blakemore, Erin. "The Secret Student Group That Stood Up to the Nazis." *Smithsonian Magazine*, February 27, 2017. SmithsonianMag.com/smart-news/the-secret-student -group-stood-up-nazis-180962250.

Branigan, Tania. "China's Great Famine: The True Story." *The Guardian*, January 1, 2013. TheGuardian.com/world/2013/jan/01 /china-great-famine-book-tombstone.

Buckley, Chris, and Didi Kirsten Tatlow. "Cultural Revolution Shaped Xi Jinping, From Schoolboy to Survivor." *The New York Times*, September 24, 2015. NYTimes.com/2015/09/25/world /asia/xi-jinping-china-cultural-revolution.html.

Colitt, Leslie. "Berlin Crisis: The Standoff at Checkpoint Charlie." *The Guardian*, October 24, 2011. TheGuardian.com /world/2011/oct/24/berlin-crisis-standoff-checkpoint -charlie.

Dunbar, Brian. "July 20, 1969: One Giant Leap for Mankind." NASA.gov, July 15, 2019. NASA.gov/mission_pages/apollo /apollo11.html.

Gjelten, Tom. "Boundlessly Idealistic, Universal Declaration of Human Rights Is Still Resisted." *NPR*, December 10, 2018. NPR.org/2018/12/10/675210421/its-human-rights-day -however-its-not-universally-accepted.

Hammer, Joshua. "In Northern Ireland, Getting Past the Troubles." *Smithsonian Magazine*, March 9, 2009. SmithsonianMag .com/travel/in-northern-ireland-getting-past-the-troubles -52862004.

History.com Editors. "Atomic Bomb History." *History.com*, A&E Television Networks. Updated February 21, 2020. History.com/topics/world-war-ii/atomic-bomb-history.

_____. 2011. "Collapse of the Soviet Union." *History.com*, A&E Television Networks. Updated September 11, 2020. History.com /topics/cold-war/fall-of-soviet-union.

_____. 2009. "First World Cup." *History.com*, A&E Television Networks. Updated July 28, 2019. History.com/this-day -in-history/first-world-cup.

_____. 2009. "Jawaharlal Nehru." *History.com*, A&E Television Networks. Updated August 21, 2018. History.com/topics /india/jawaharlal-nehru.

_____. 2009. "Long March." *History.com*, A&E Television Networks. Updated August 21, 2018. History.com/topics /china/long-march.

_____. 2010. "The Space Race." *History.com*, A&E Television Networks. Updated February 21, 2020. History.com /topics/cold-war/space-race.

_____. 2018. "United Nations." *History.com*, A&E Television Networks. Updated August 21, 2018. History.com/topics /world-war-ii/united-nations.

"History of HIV and AIDS Overview." *Avert*. Updated October 10, 2019. Avert.org/professionals/history-hiv-aids/overview.

Kuhn, Anthony. "Chinese Red Guards Apologize, Reopening a Dark Chapter." *All Things Considered*, NPR, February 4, 2014. NPR.org/sections/parallels/2014/01/23/265228870 /chinese-red-guards-apologize-reopening-a-dark-chapter.

PBS. "'Kristallnacht.'" *American Experience: America and the Holocaust*, Public Broadcasting Service, March 1, 2021. PBS.org /wgbh/americanexperience/features/holocaust-kristallnacht.

Wiener Holocaust Library. n.d. "The Early Years of the Nazi Party." *The Holocaust Explained*. Accessed March 1, 2021. TheHolocaustExplained.org/the-nazi-rise-to-power /the-early-years-of-the-nazi-party/what-were-hitlers-ideas.

ACKNOWLEDGMENTS

Thank you to my editors, Barbara Isenberg and Leila Sales—your keen insights were invaluable. Thank you to Nicole, Zachary, Benjamin, and Eva for your constant love and support.

ABOUT THE AUTHOR

Judy Dodge Cummings is the author of many books for children and teenagers. A former high school teacher, she holds an MFA in creative writing for children and teenagers from Hamline University. Judy writes both nonfiction and fiction, and her goal is to transport young readers back in time. Judy lives in south central Wisconsin with her dog, three cats, and too many books to count.

Printed in the USA
CPSIA information can be obtained
at www.ICGtesting.com
CBHW040740280124
3678CB00006B/47

9 781648 767616